Bullshit Secret

Hilarious Swear Word Coloring Book

for Fun & Stress Releasing

Charles C. Golden

Happy Coloring!

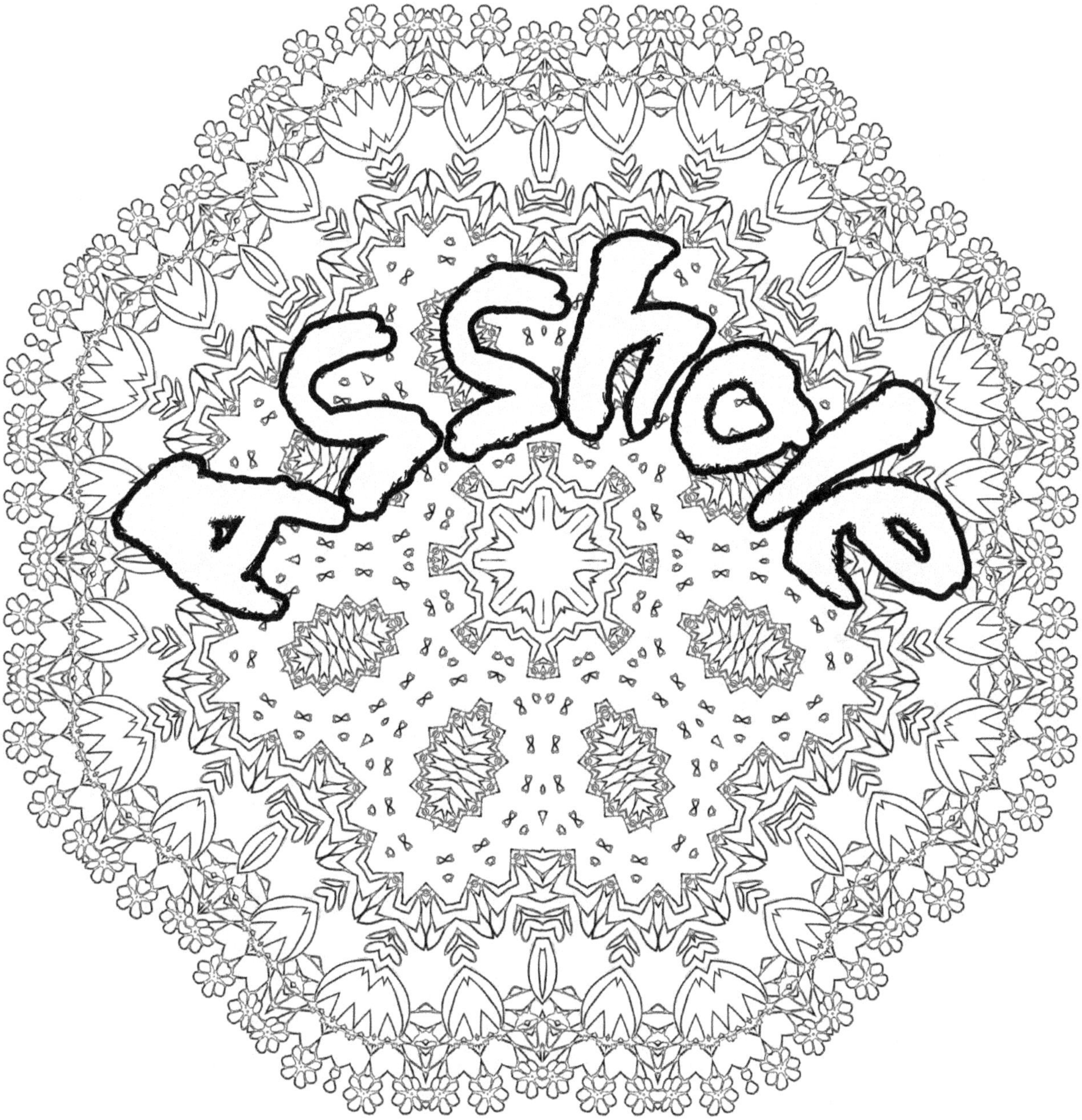
Asshole

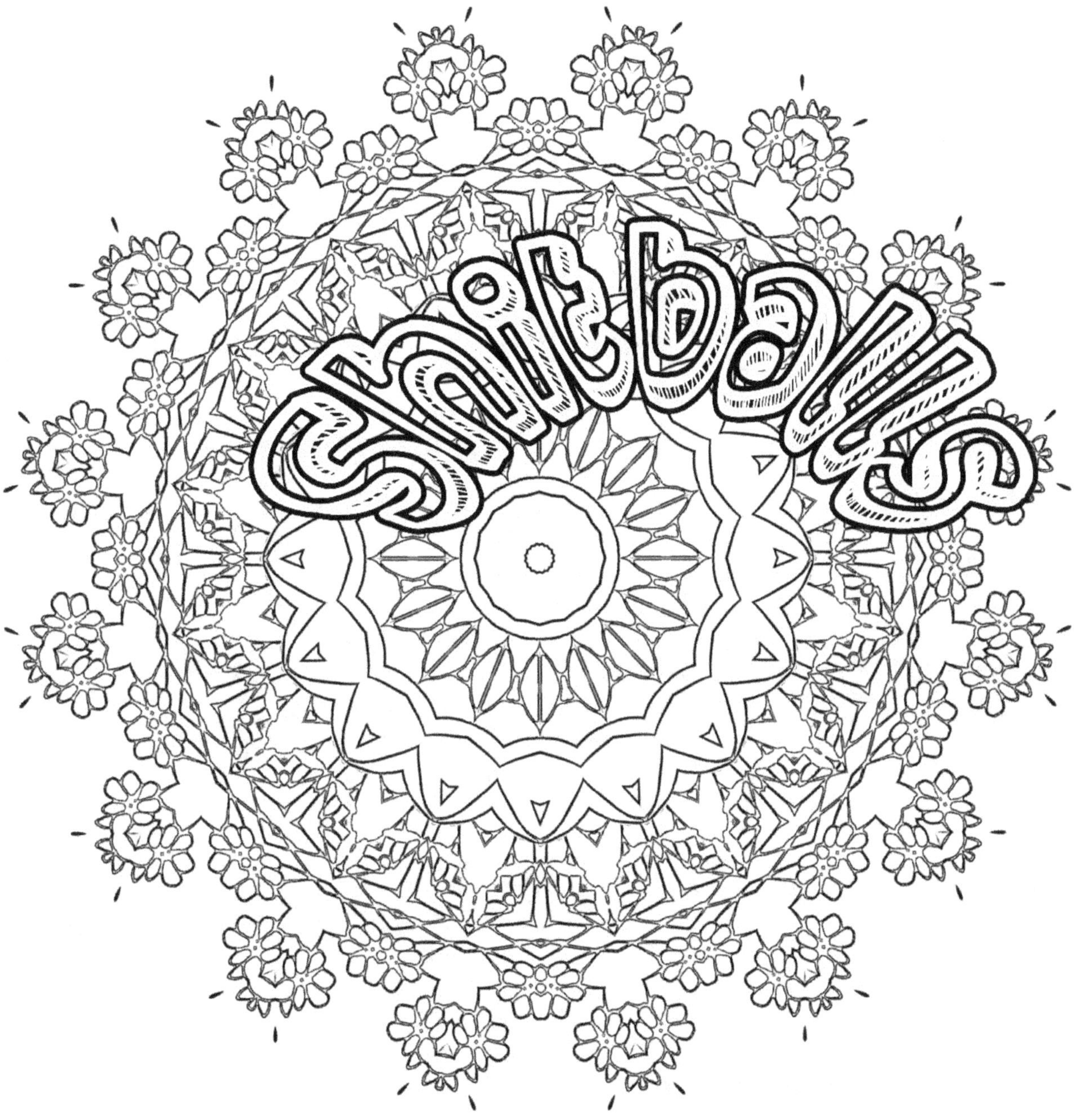
shitballs

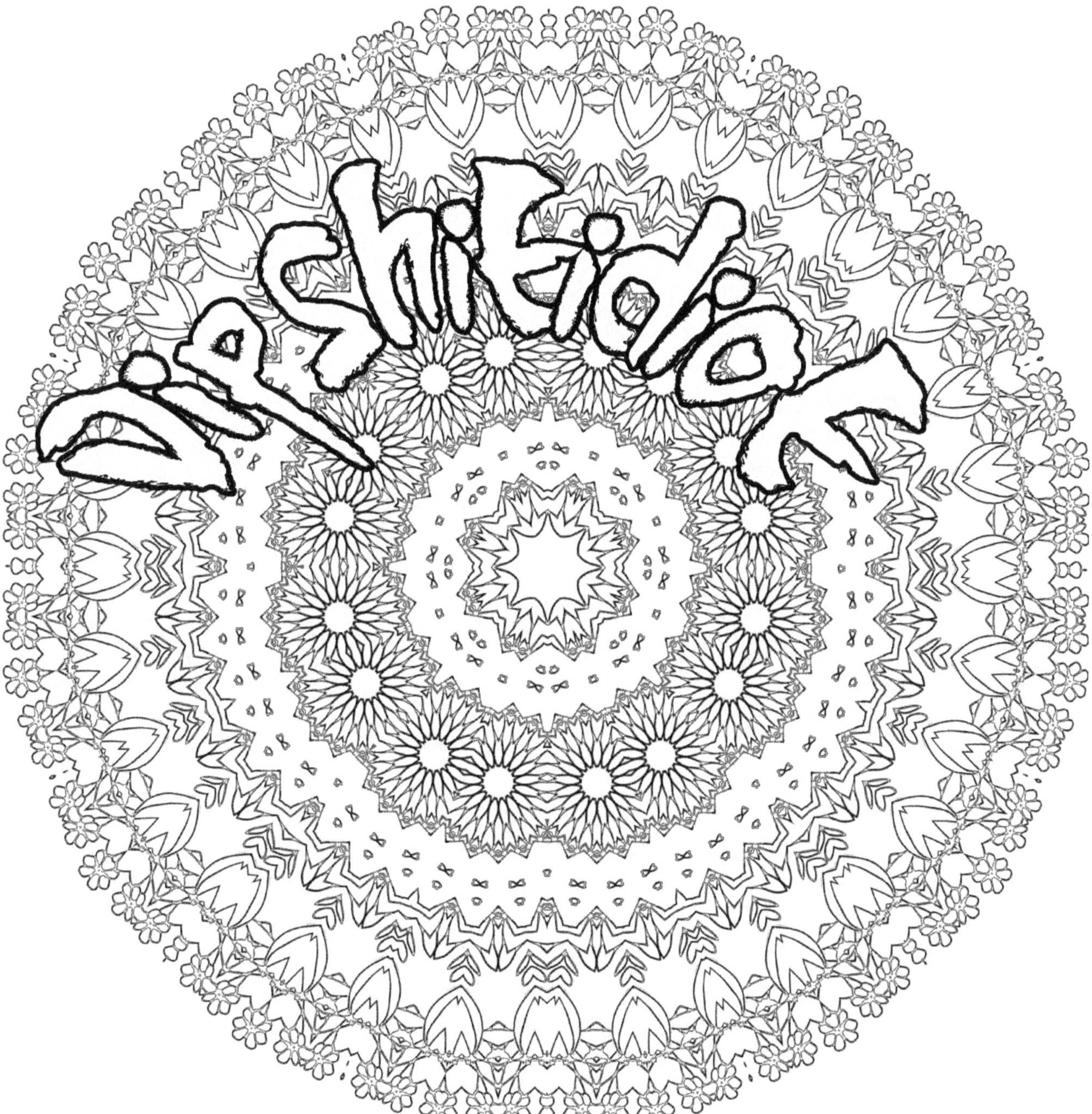
Dipshitidiot

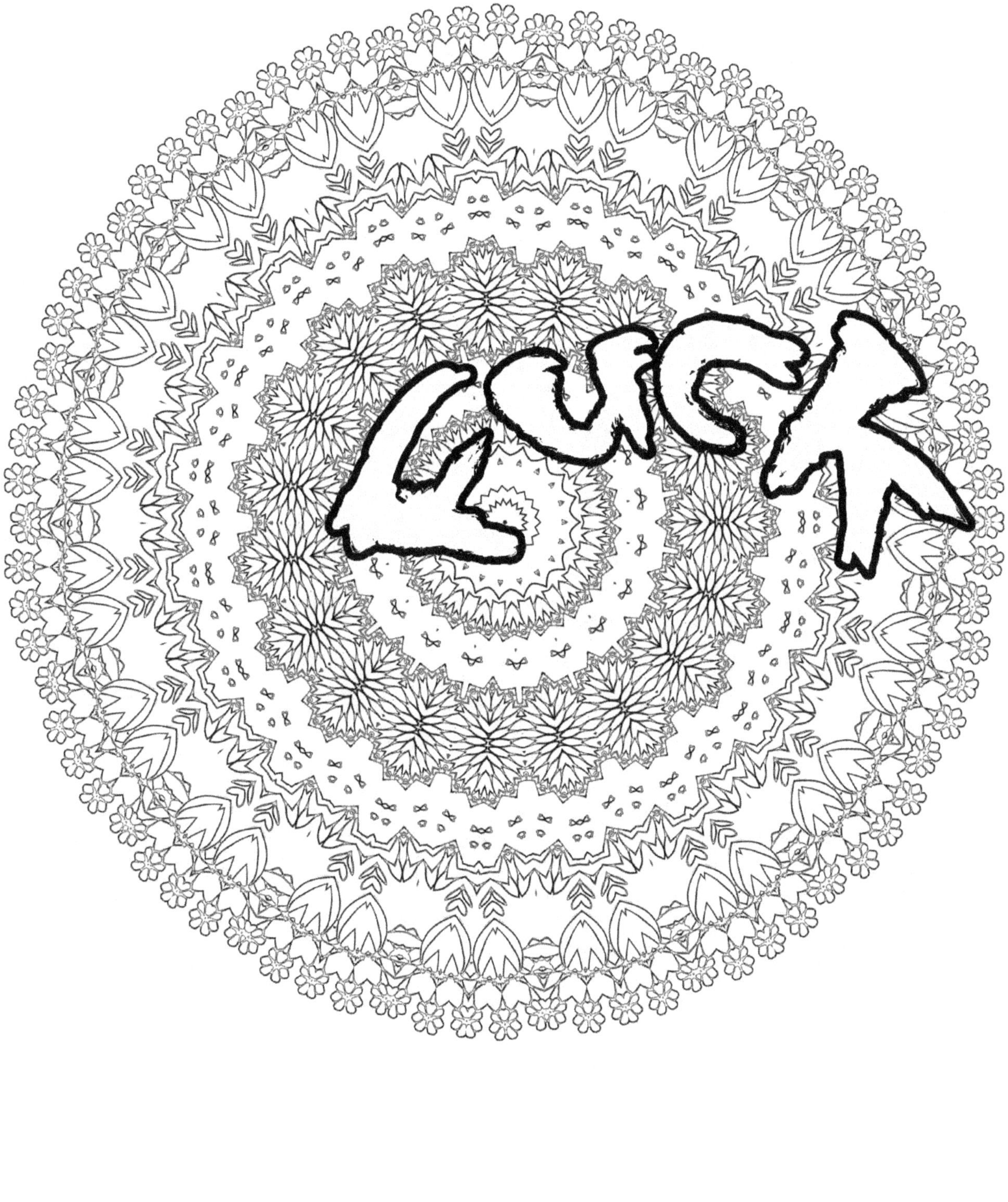
LUCK

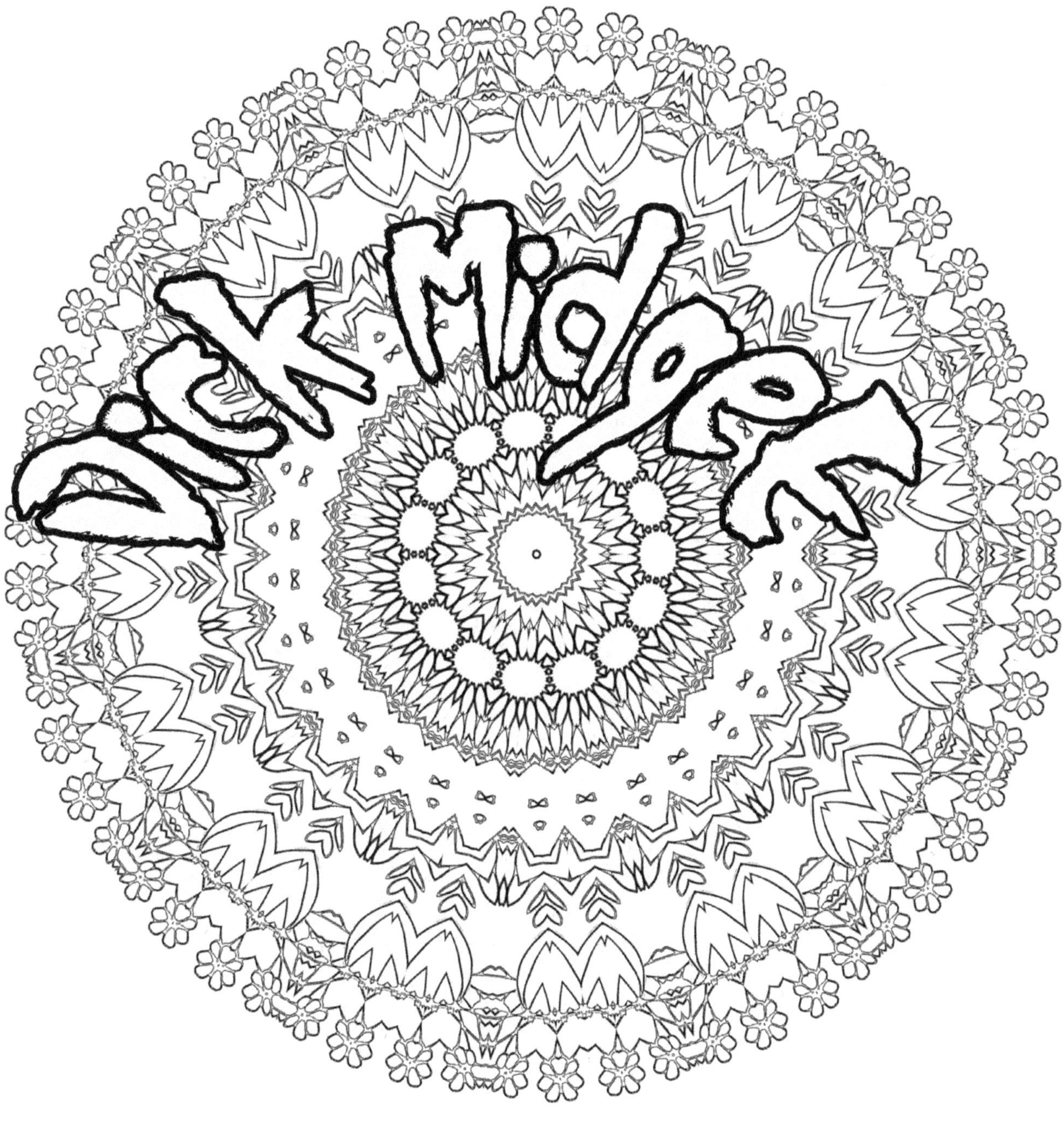
Dick Midget

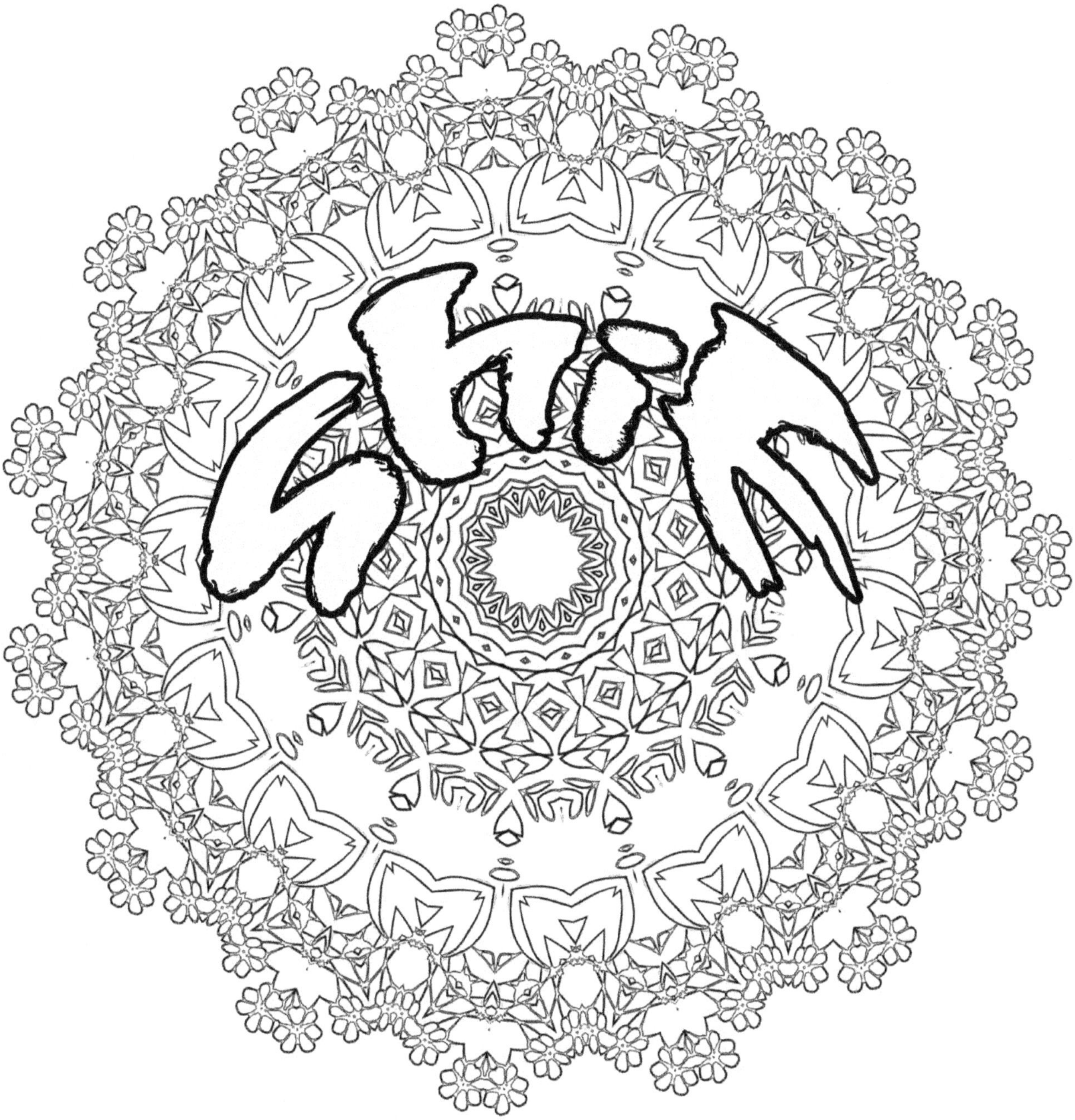

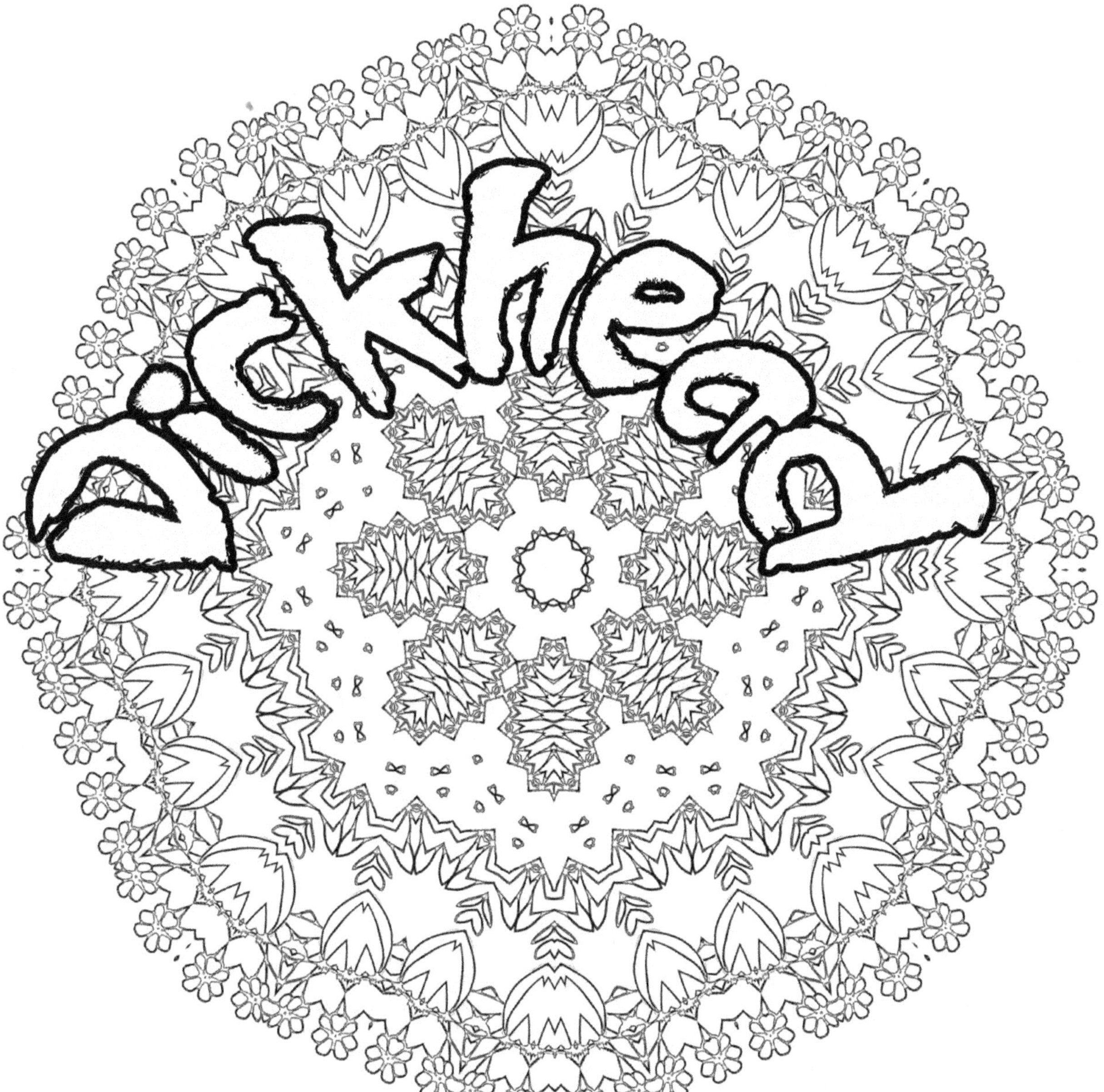
Dickhead

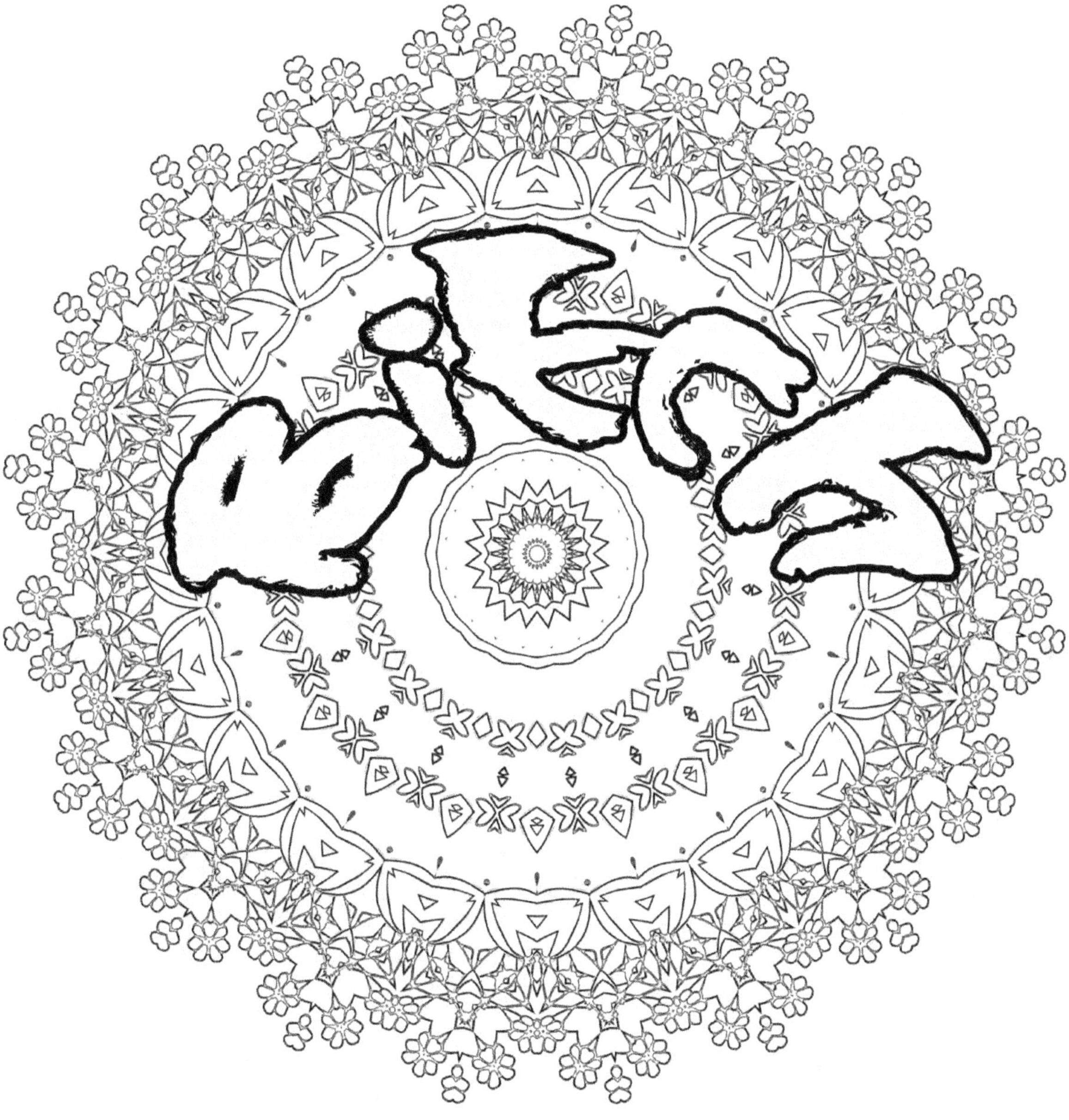

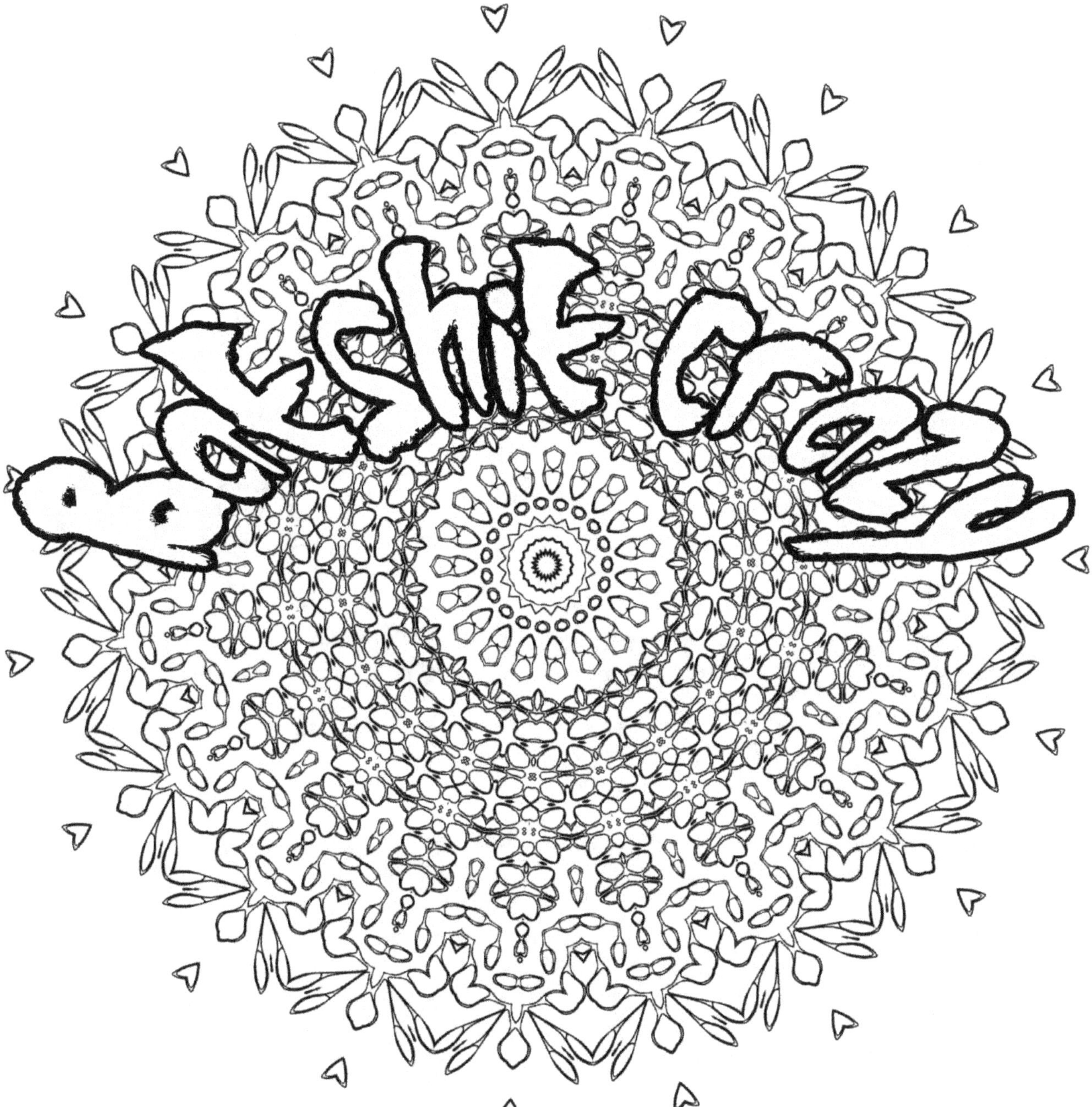
Batshit crazy

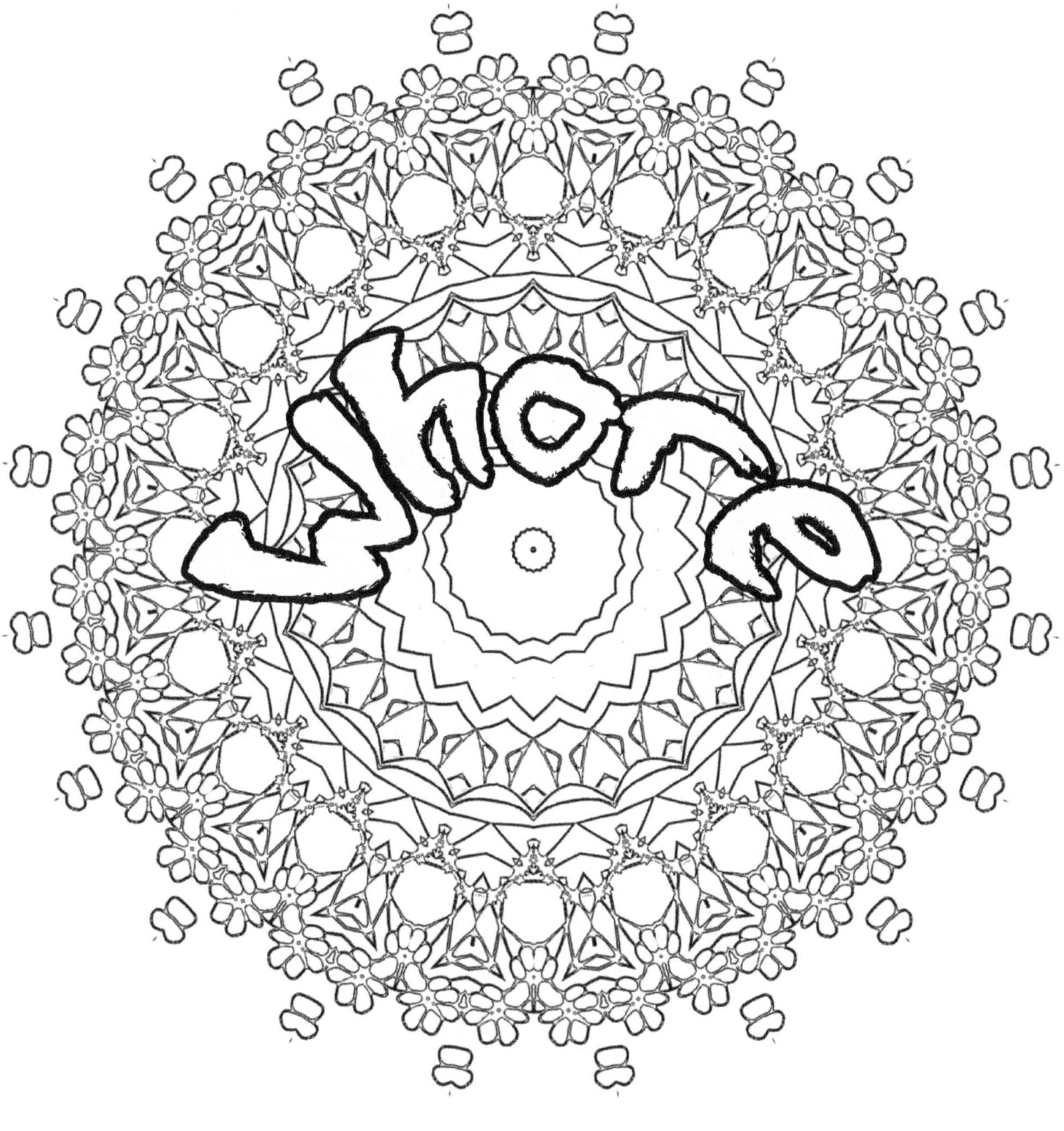
whore

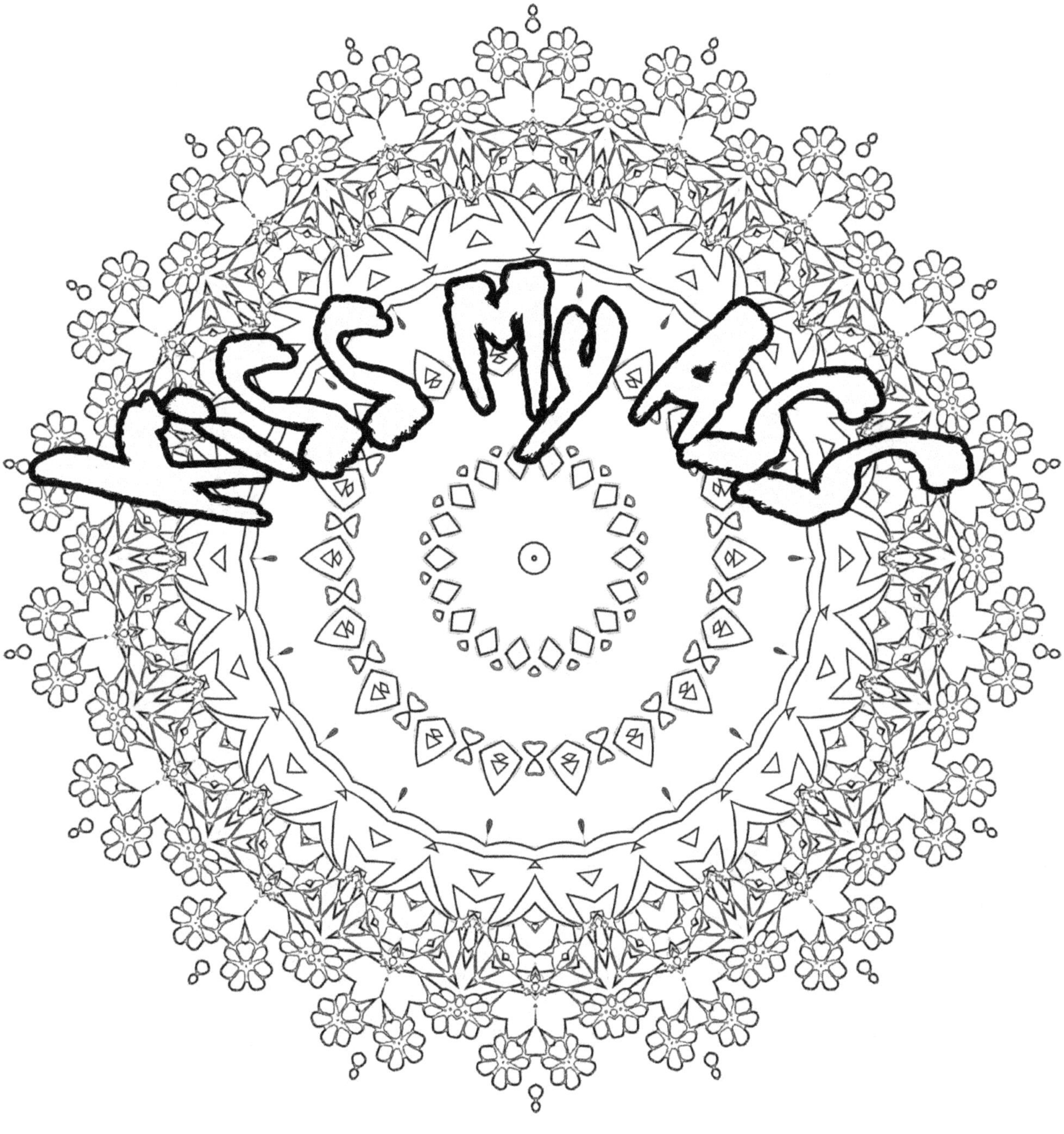
KISS MY ASS

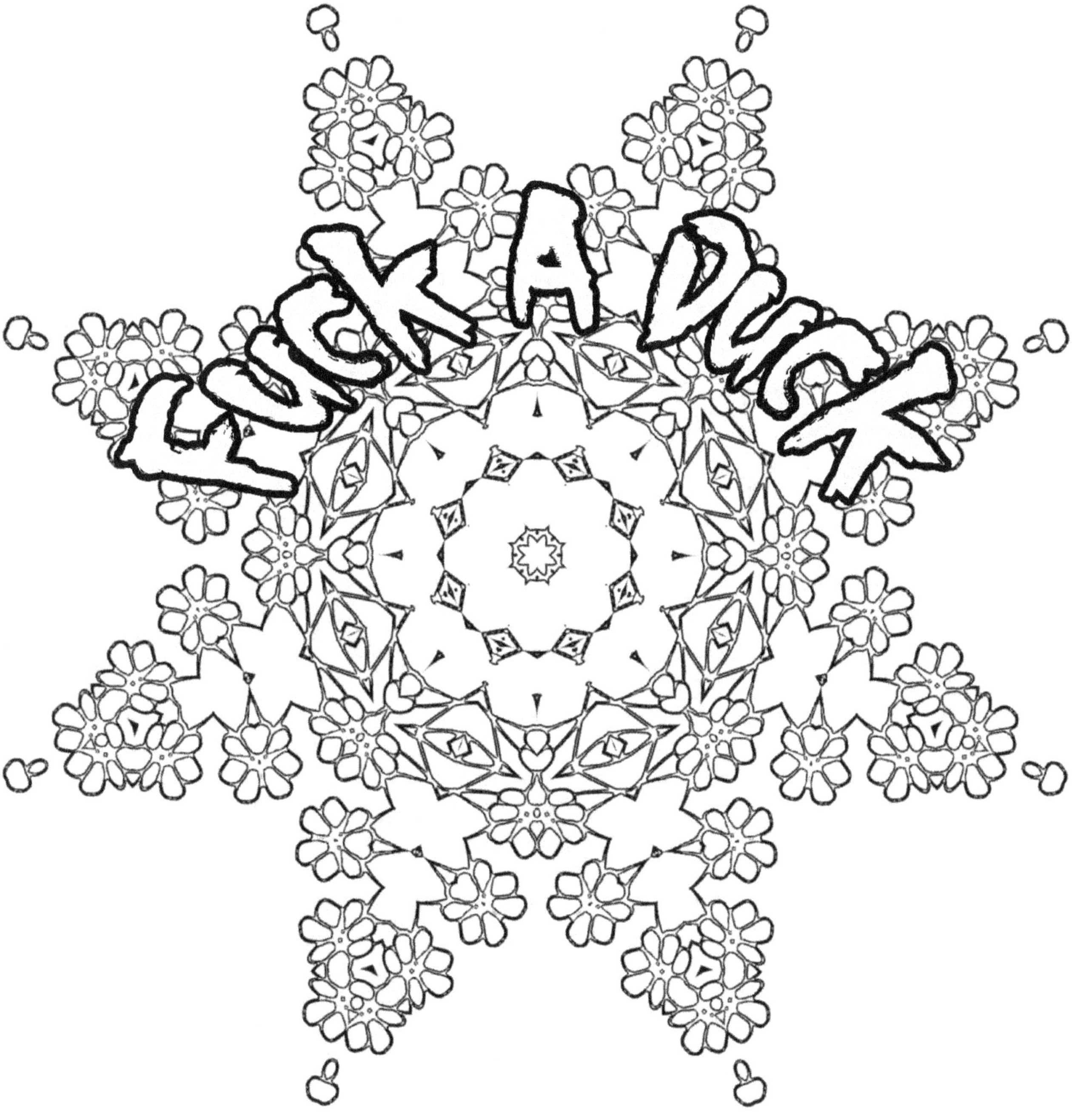
FUCK A DUCK

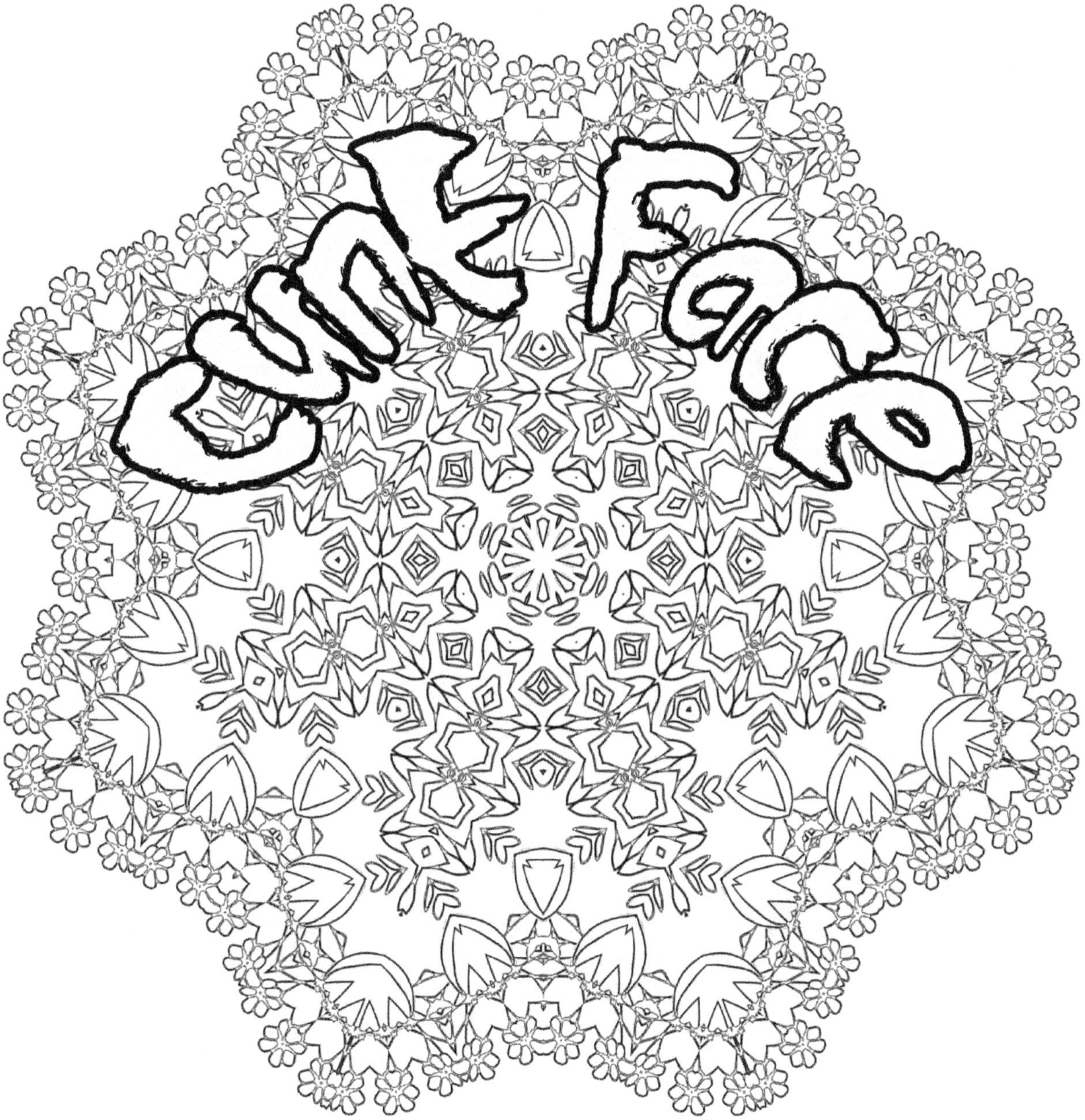
Cunt Face

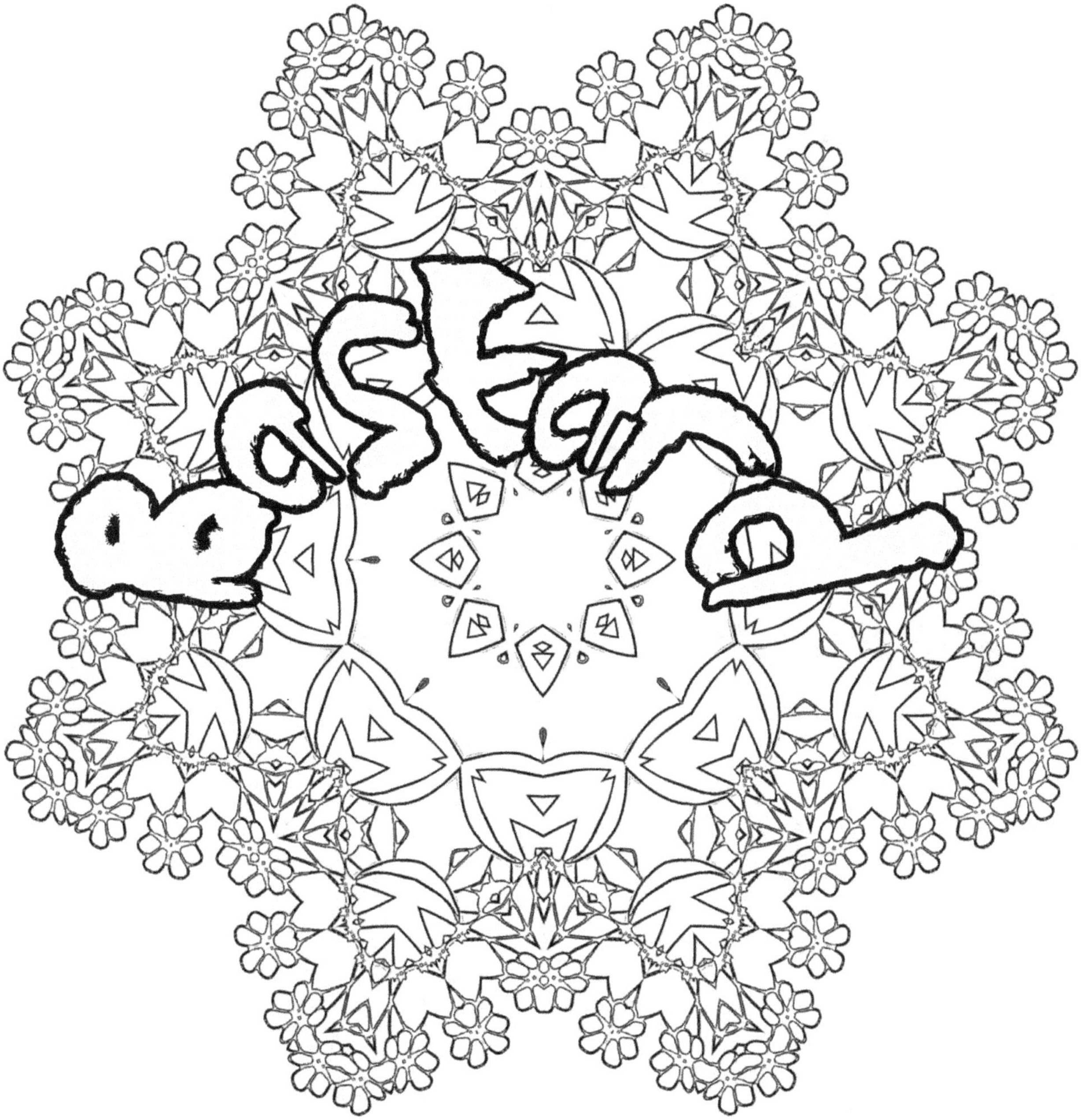
Bastard

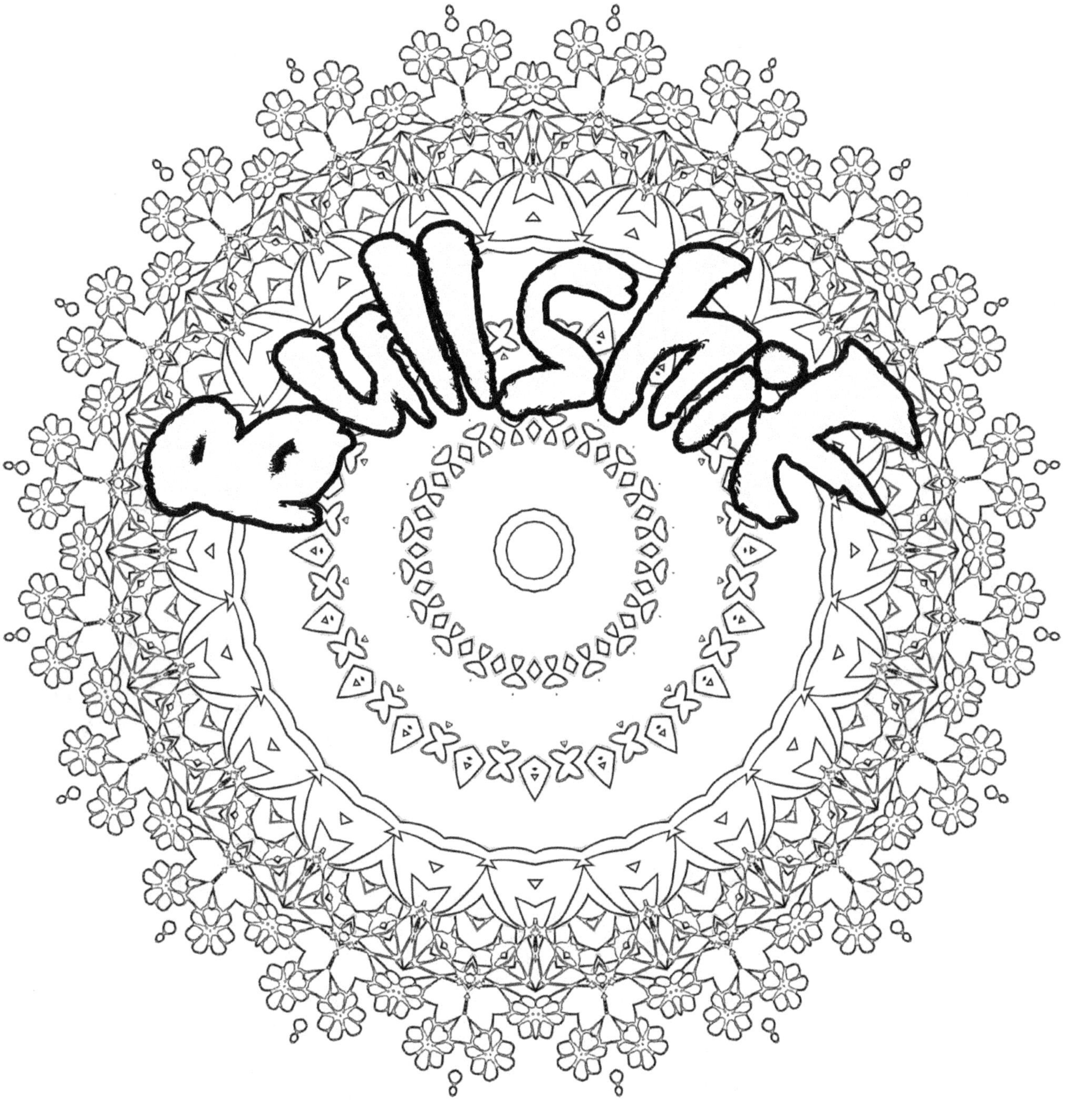
Bullshit

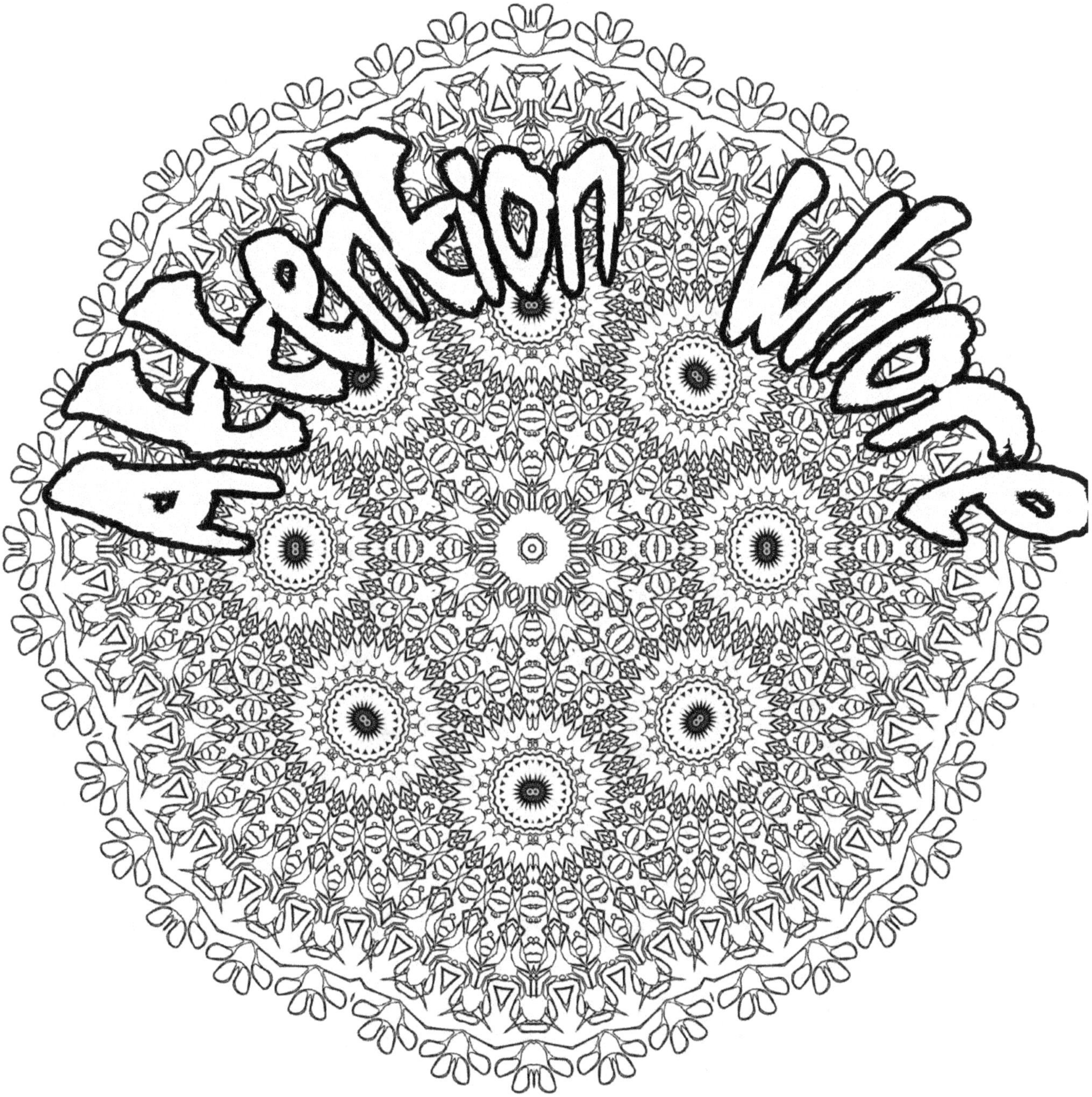
Attention Whore

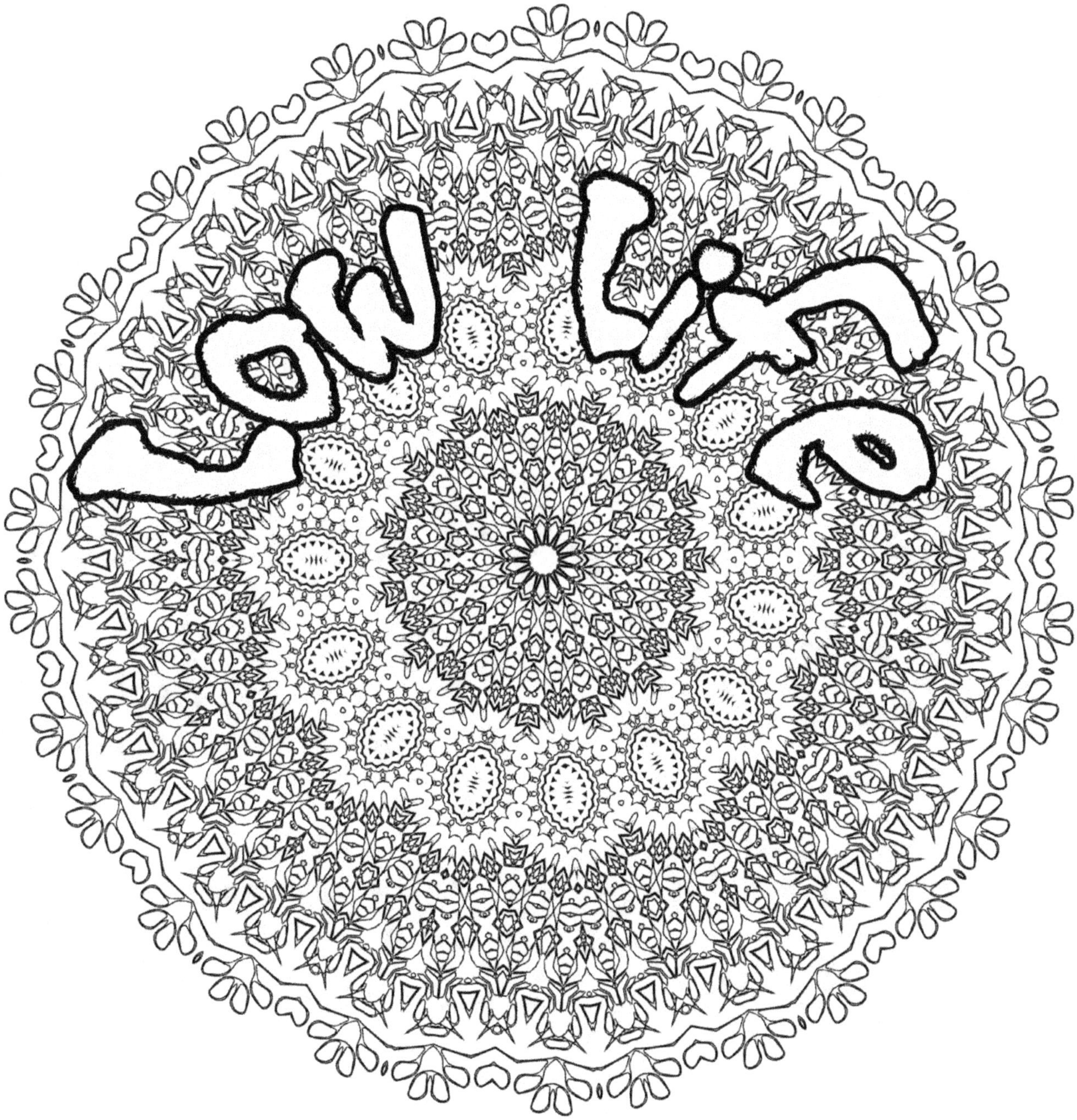
Low Life

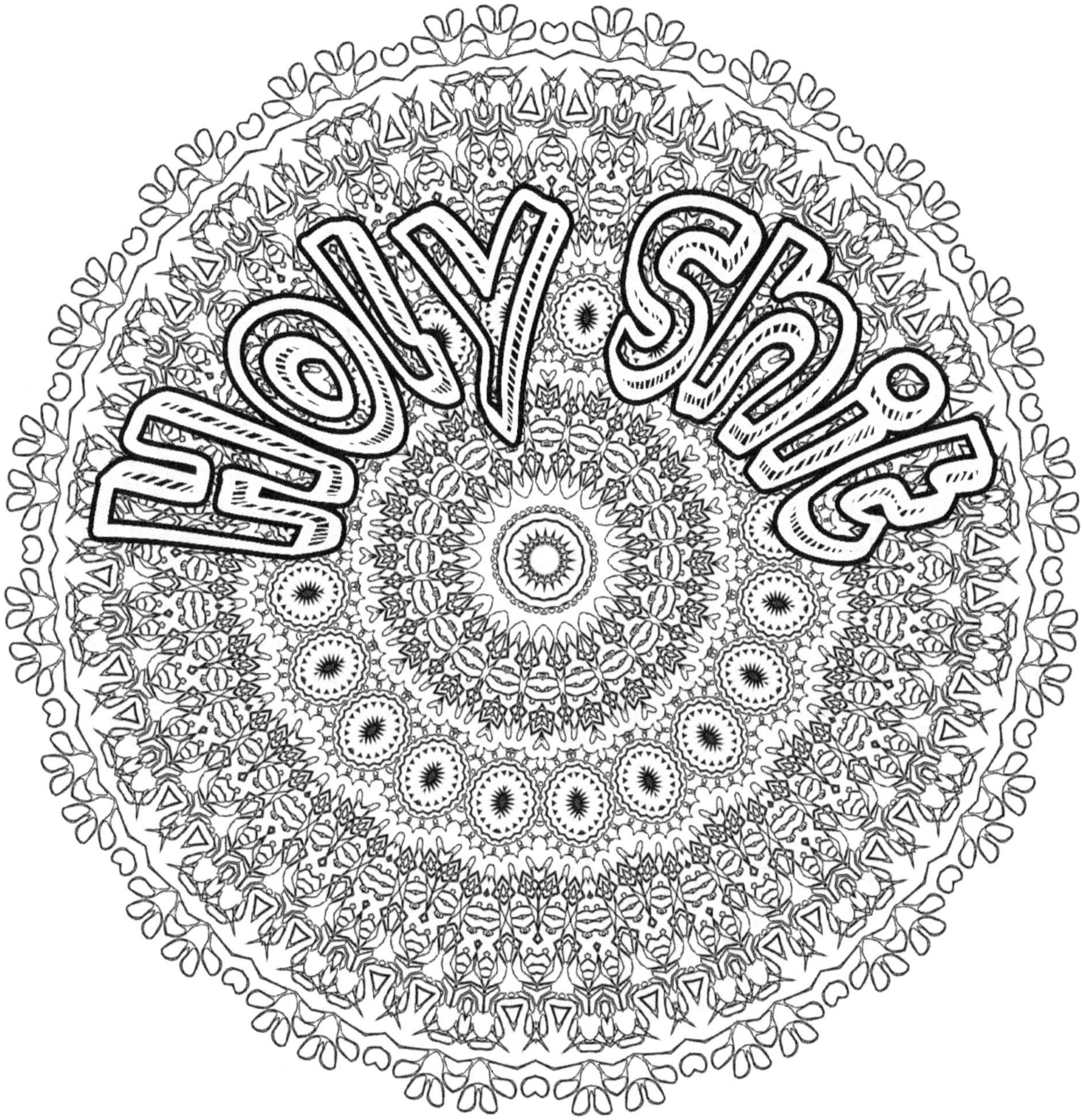
Holy Shit

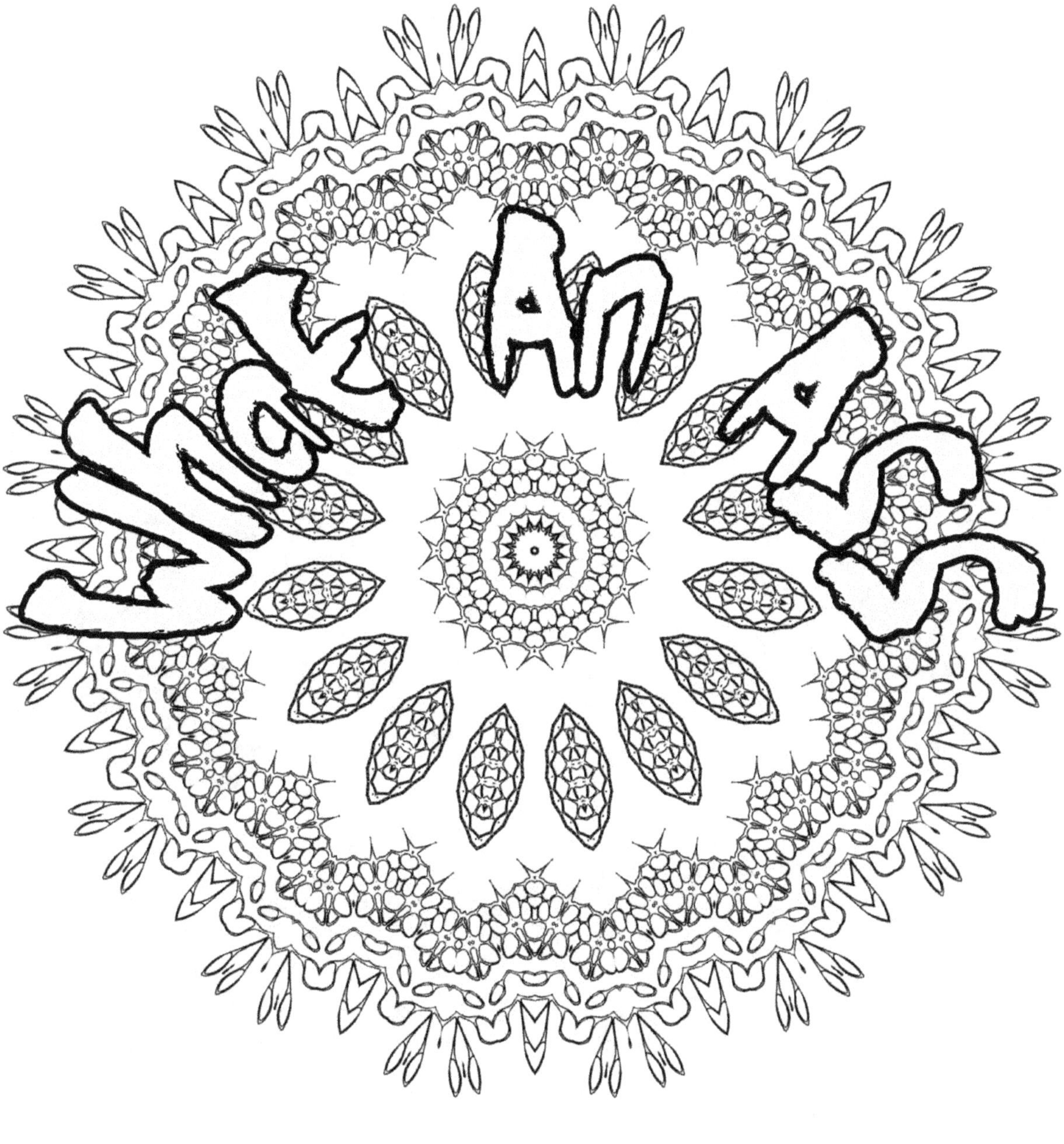
What An Ass

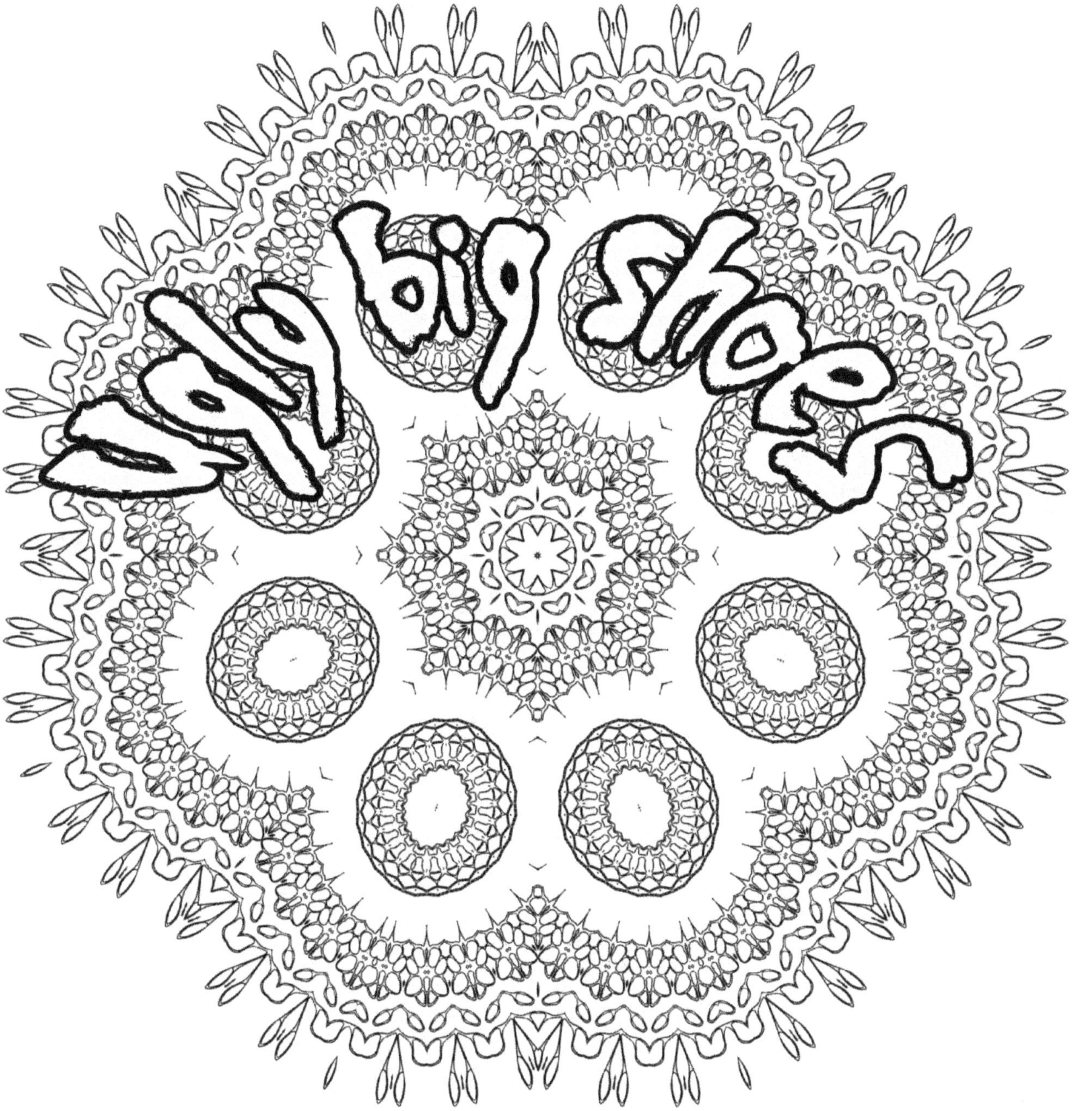
ugly big shoes

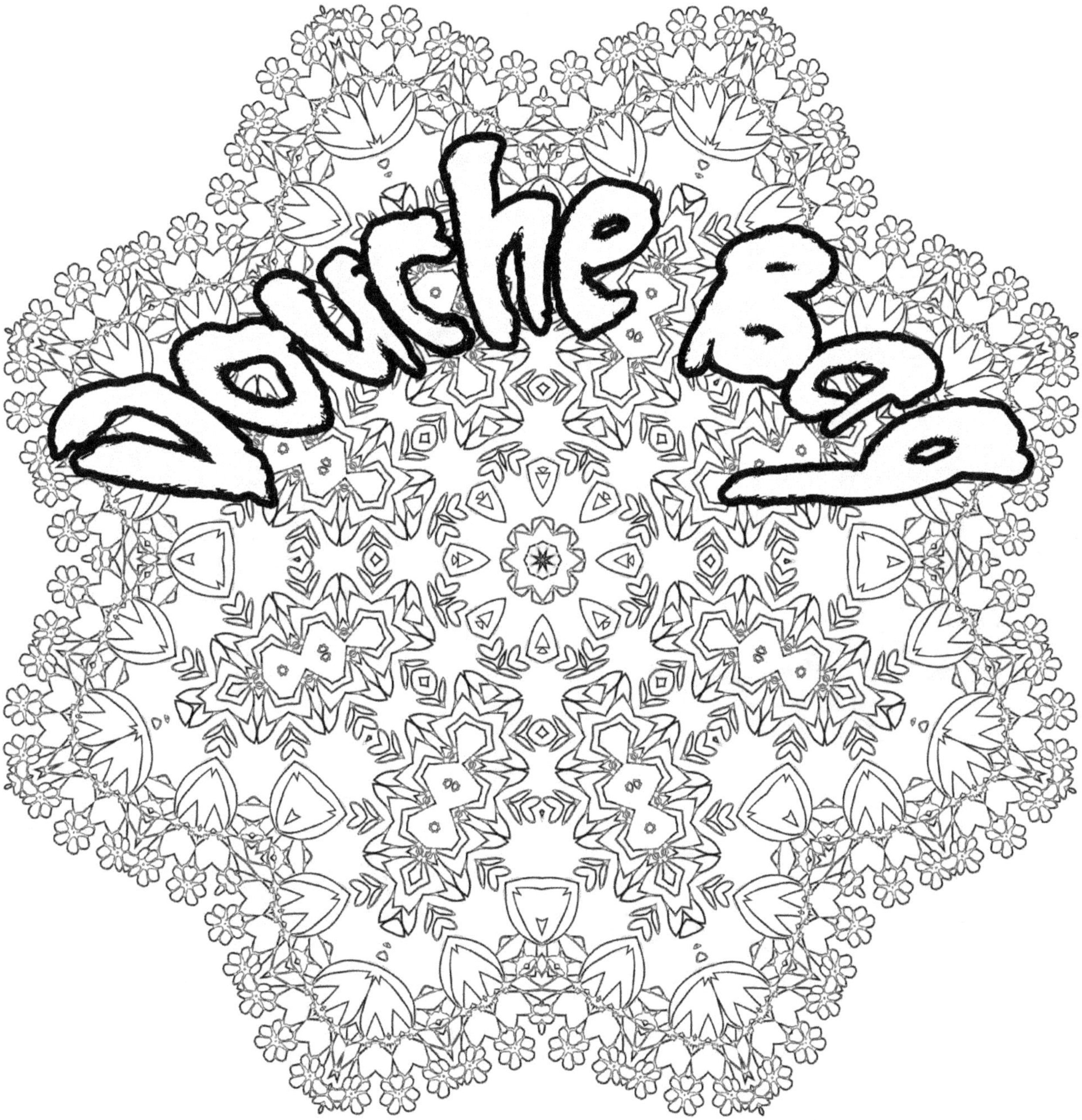
Douche Bag

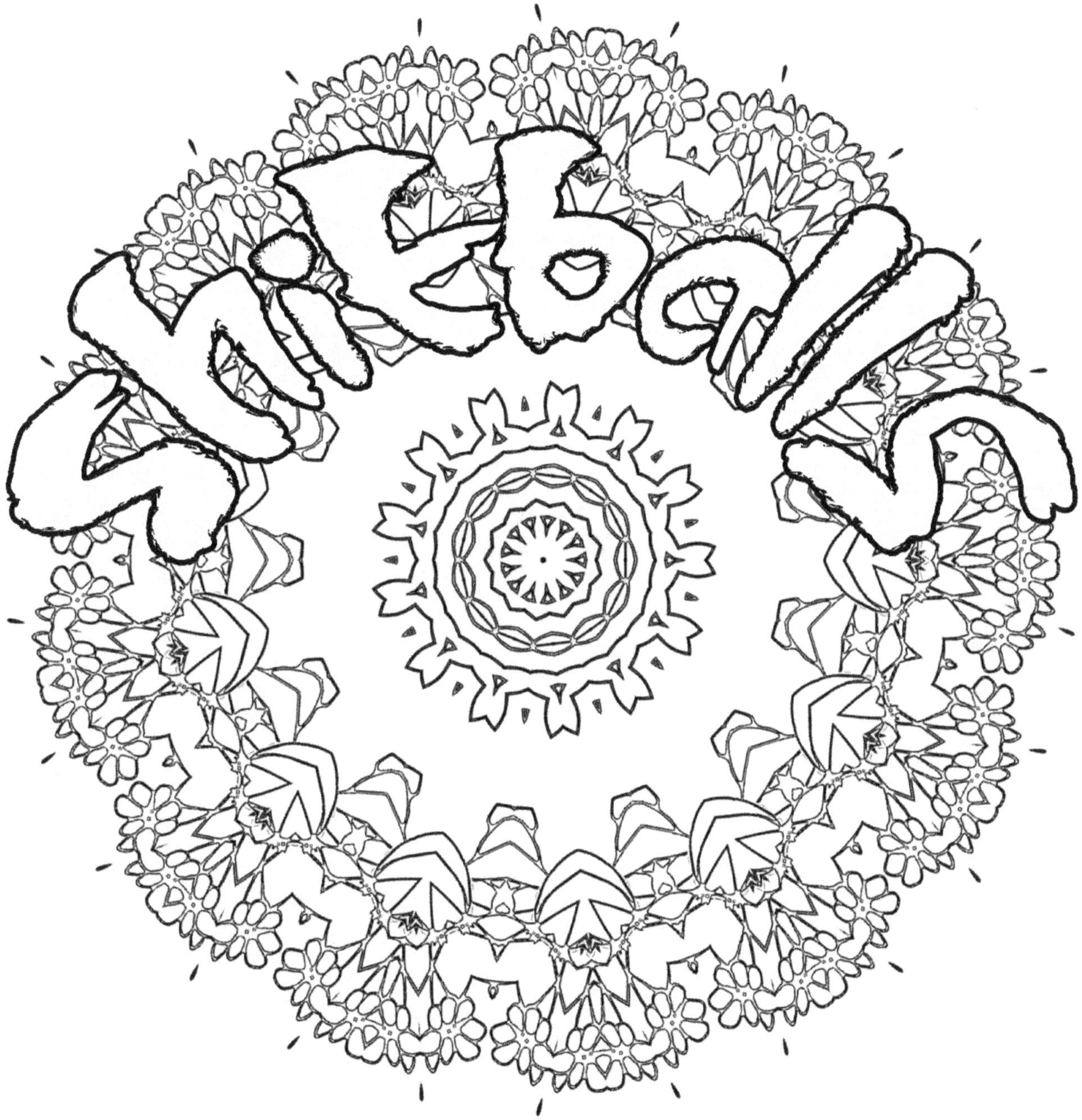
shitballs

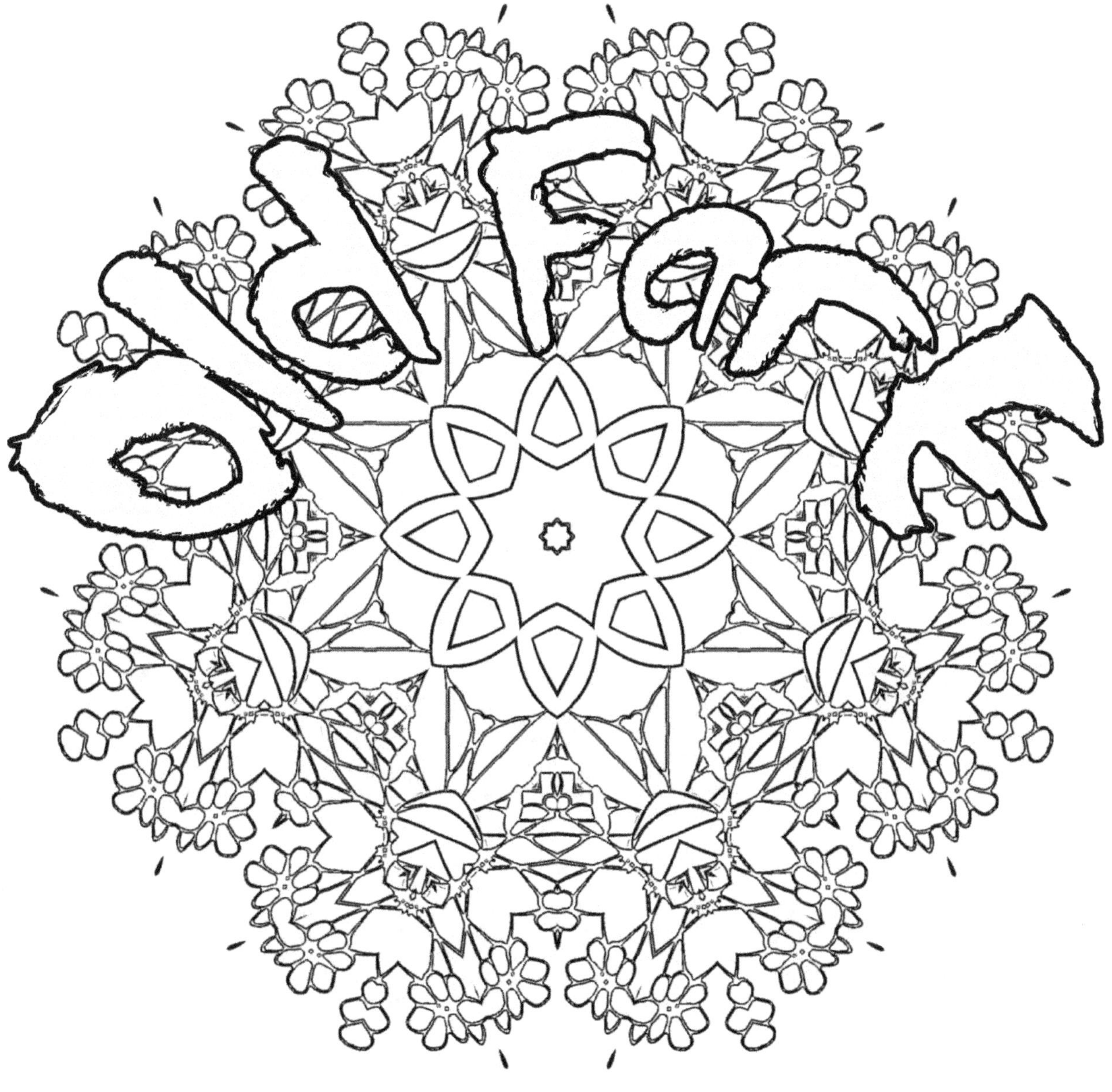
old Fart

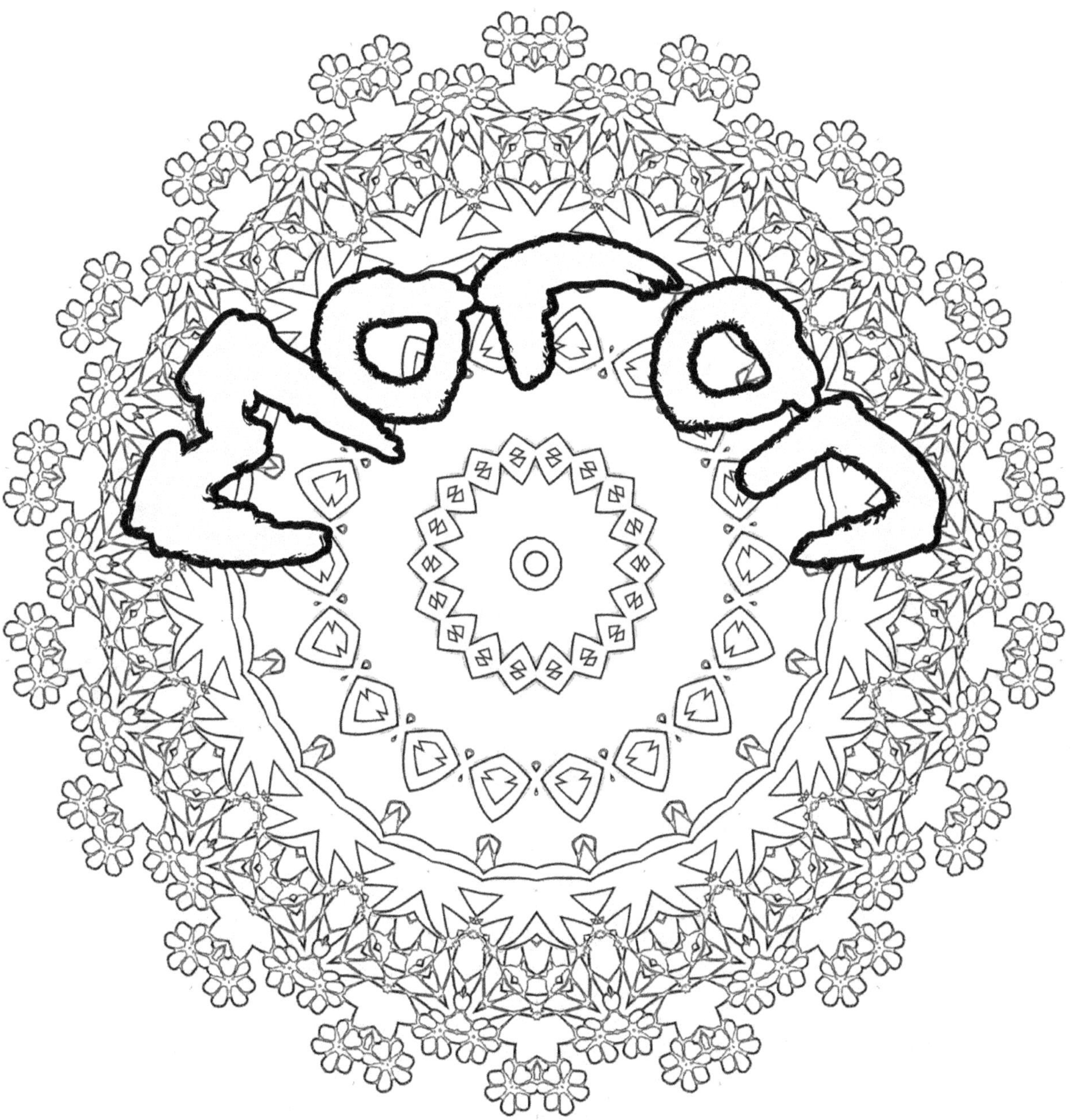

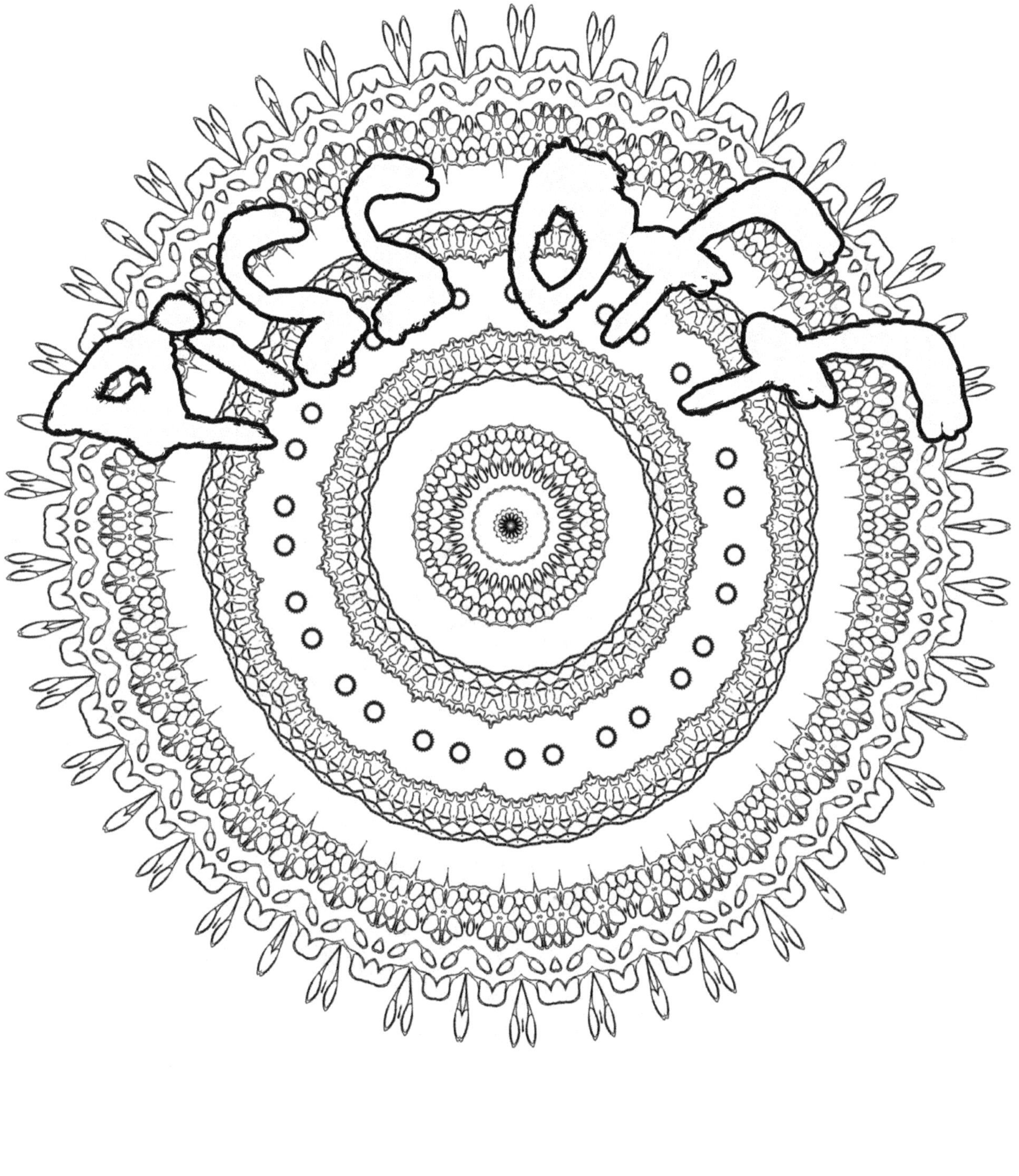

www.ingramcontent.com/pod-product-compliance
Lightning Source LLC
Chambersburg PA
CBHW081130180526
45170CB00008B/3062